T0345940

THE COVENANT

AND

THE CHARTER

BY

J. L. BRIERLY, D.C.L., LL.M.

Chichele Professor of International Law and
Fellow of All Souls College, Oxford

The Henry Sidgwick Memorial Lecture
delivered at Newnham College, Cambridge
on 30 November 1946

CAMBRIDGE

AT THE UNIVERSITY PRESS

1947

CAMBRIDGE
UNIVERSITY PRESS

University Printing House, Cambridge CB2 8BS, United Kingdom

Published in the United States of America by Cambridge University Press, New York

Cambridge University Press is part of the University of Cambridge.

It furthers the University's mission by disseminating knowledge in the pursuit of education, learning and research at the highest international levels of excellence.

www.cambridge.org
Information on this title: www.cambridge.org/9781107663886

© Cambridge University Press 1947

First published 1947
Re-issued 2014

A catalogue record for this publication is available from the British Library

ISBN 978-1-107-66388-6 Paperback

The Covenant and the Charter

IN these early days of the United Nations there is a risk that a comparison between the Covenant and the Charter may not be altogether fair. We know now most of what we shall ever know about the Covenant, because the history of the League is now a closed chapter, and it tells us how the Covenant worked in practice. But in a sense we do not yet know much about the Charter, because the text of a document is never a very safe guide to an understanding of the institution to which it relates. Constitutions always have to be interpreted and applied, and in the process they are overlaid with precedents and conventions which change them after a time into something very different from what anyone, with only the original text before him, could possibly have foreseen. The Covenant underwent a process of this kind, and we must expect the Charter to do the same. Apart from the text of the Charter itself we have a few months' rather confused and inconclusive experience of its working to go on. Most of us feel, I know, that that experience has so far been disappointing and even alarming, but it is too early yet to be discouraged. Even if the start has been unpropitious, we must never forget that for the time being, and probably for a long time to come, our only hope of a better international order is somehow to make the Charter work in its present form. Criticism of it therefore should be tentative and provisional, and it should try to be constructive.

It would be impossible in a single lecture to examine in any detail the points of similarity and of difference in the Covenant and the Charter. The similarities were inevitable, because the purposes of the League and of the United Nations are fundamentally the same. The Covenant stated the purposes of the League with its usual economy of words as being 'to promote international co-operation and to achieve international peace and security'; and the Charter says much the same at greater length. The draftsmen had no real choice, for these are the two great purposes to which any general international organization whatsoever is bound to be directed. But the differences are very numerous too. The Charter makes an obvious and rather childish attempt to get away from the associations of the Covenant even in small points of terminology, such as the substitution of the Security Council for the Council, of the General Assembly for the Assembly, and of the Trustee-ship system for the system of Mandates. I intend, however, in this lecture to confine myself to differences which seem to me to be based on important differences of principle. I shall have very little to say, therefore, about the social and economic side of the two organizations. It is generally recognized that in this field the League had a large measure of success, and that the methods that it used were not open to serious criticism. It is evidently intended that in the main the United Nations should carry on the work with perhaps some improvements of organization, such as the establishment of the Economic and Social Council, but without any change of principle.

The important innovations which the Charter has introduced begin to appear as soon as we remind ourselves of the reasons which were thought to make it necessary to create a new organization instead of reviving and continuing the League. I know that there were political causes which would have made that difficult in any case, but there was also a general feeling that the League had failed because it was not strong enough for its task. It was to correct the supposed weakness of the League as a system of security that a new and stronger body had to be created, and in a sense the feeling was justified. The League had not been strong enough to deal with the aggressions, first of Japan, then of Italy, and finally of Germany. But most of the critics did not inquire very deeply into the causes of the League's weakness, though they were not far to seek. When a great experiment has failed it is easy to salve our consciences by attributing the failure to some defect in the original design for which others, and not we, were responsible, rather than to the manner in which we ourselves have carried out our obligations to make it succeed. I think that is what the critics did. For there is no need to look for an explanation beyond the plain fact that of the seven Great Powers upon whose support the League necessarily depended for success one stood aside from the first, one was in a state of chaos and was left out in the cold, three repudiated everything for which the League stood, and the other two, whose burden had thus been made unexpectedly heavy, were, not without some excuse, never more than half-hearted in the support which they gave to it. That the League failed to deal with the aggressions of the inter-war period cannot, therefore, fairly be held to prove anything one way or the other about the merits of the Covenant, for, if the circumstances had been the same, it would have failed just as certainly if the Covenant had been the most perfect document ever drafted.

But of course that only proves that, as events turned out, it was not any weakness in the Covenant that led to the failure. It may still be true, as the founders of the United Nations evidently thought, that the League was based on a wrong principle which would have made it fail even if the circumstances had been more favourable. The principle of the Covenant is very simple. It was intended that it should create a system of co-operation between States, which were to retain their sovereignty but to agree to do and not to do certain things in the exercise of their sovereign rights. The Covenant did not contain even the beginnings of a system of international government in the proper sense of the word 'government'. I remember in the early days of the League meeting a member of Parliament who had just returned from a first visit to Geneva. He said he had discovered that the League was not 'it' but 'they', and he was perfectly right. As a corporate body there was hardly anything that the League could do; in fact, there is, I think, only one Article in the Covenant which envisages action by the League as such at all, and I suspect that this provision was a mere slip of drafting. Article XI does say that in the event of war or any threat of war 'the League shall take any action that may be deemed wise and effectual to safeguard the peace of nations', but elsewhere throughout the Covenant it is normally 'the members of the League' who undertake to act in some particular way in a certain event, and so far as I know the departure from the usual terminology in Article XI had no special significance in the practice of the League.

Now it is clear that an association, whether of individuals or of States, which is nothing but a name for the members collectively, cannot, as an association, be otherwise than weak. It may be effective for its purposes, but that will depend on the conduct of the members individually, upon their ability and willingness to honour the obligations they may have undertaken; they cannot be made to act together, and a majority of them cannot decide or act for the whole body. Hence, if we want an association to be strong, it is a right instinct which urges us to exchange the co-operative basis of the association for one that is organic. But that cannot be done merely by giving the association a new constitution, just as you cannot turn a nation into a democracy merely by giving it democratic institutions to work. In both cases you need also certain other conditions which cannot be hastily improvised, and the most vital question which the Charter seems to me to raise is whether we yet have in the international field the conditions which are needed in order to make an organic international institution work. I do not think we have.

If you compare the Preamble of the Covenant with the 'Purposes' of the United Nations in Article I of the Charter, you will see how the Charter has taken a first step, a rather hesitating first step it is true, away from the purely co-operative basis of international organization. All the emphasis in the Covenant is on what the High Contracting Parties, that is to say, the members of the League, are to do; they are to accept obligations not to resort to war, to follow prescriptions of open, just and honourable relations between nations, to respect treaty obligations, and so on. In the Charter on the other hand the 'Purposes' are those of the United Nations, and the context shows that this means the Organization as a whole and not its members severally. The same contrast runs all through the two documents. It is, I think, one of the reasons why the Charter had to be a much longer document than the Covenant—it has III Articles against the Covenant's 26—though the greater length is also partly due to mere prolixity. The Covenant did not need to cramp the future activities of its organs by minute definitions of their respective functions; it could say quite generally that either the Assembly or the

Council was to be able to 'deal with any matter within the sphere of action of the League or affecting the peace of the world', and leave them to adjust their relations with one another, as they did, as experience accumulated. Thus for the organization as a body it contained the mere outlines of a constitution, and its prescriptions only became precise and detailed when it proceeded to define the obligations which the members were undertaking. The scheme of the Charter had to be exactly the reverse of this. It strictly defines the respective spheres of the Security Council and of the General Assembly, for there had to be no overlapping, and it makes the distinction turn on the separation of matters relating to security from those relating to social and economic problems. That, unfortunately, disregards the important fact that these problems are often the causes of international friction and so are not really separable from questions of security, and it also makes it more difficult than it need have been for the Security Council, with little or no work of a constructive character to do, to develop that corporate spirit which was found so valuable in the League. The obligations of the members on the other hand are stated in very general terms. They are merely to observe the 'Principles' which are contained in Article II; to fulfil their obligations in good faith, to settle their disputes peacefully, to refrain from the threat or use of force, and so on. The members in fact are given little more than a string of platitudes to guide their conduct.

The contrast is especially striking and, I think, unfortunate in the Articles which deal with the settlement of disputes and with enforcement action. Articles XII to XV of the Covenant prescribe clearly and in detail the procedures which the members of the League are to follow in order to reach a peaceful settlement, and they contain a valuable safeguard against any attempt by the Council to sacrifice the just claims of a weak power to political expediency by requiring it to publish a statement of the facts and the terms of the settlement if one is reached, or its recommendations if one is not. Chapter VI of the Charter merely says that the parties are to seek a solution by some peaceful means of their own choice, and then goes on to specify in detail what the Security Council is to do in different events. So again in Article XVI of the Covenant the event upon which sanctions are to become applicable is precisely defined—resort to war by a member State in disregard of its covenants—and so are the obligations which then fall due from the other members. Whether in any particular case the event has occurred, and therefore whether the obligation has fallen due, is left to each member to decide for itself, and it is this provision, perhaps more than any other, which has been thought to point to the weakness of the whole Covenant plan of security. Certainly it does involve the risk that the members may not all decide alike, but since sanctions would never be seriously contemplated except in a very clear case, it is practically certain, provided only that States act honestly, that their decisions would be the same. Of course if they refuse to honour their obligations, the case would be different, but then in that case no system would work. At any rate on the only occasion in the League's history when the sanctions Article was applied, all the members except a few small States which were entirely under the influence of Italy did reach identical decisions, and the failure to enforce the Covenant had nothing whatever to do with the fact that the League Council had no power to make a decision on behalf of the League as a body. In Chapter VII of the Charter on the other hand the event upon which enforcement action is to be taken by the United Nations is left entirely undefined; the Security Council has only to determine that a threat to the peace or a breach of it exists or that an act of aggression has been committed, and it may then decide on behalf of the whole Organization what measures shall be taken to maintain or to restore the peace. It has been argued, I know, that it is unwise to define too clearly the occasion on which sanctions will be applied—Sir Austen Chamberlain once said that to define aggression was more likely to provide an intending aggressor with a signpost than with a warning—but the Covenant plan seems to me to avoid any such risk as that. It does not define aggression; what it does is to make a definition unnecessary by making the question turn simply upon the acceptance or the refusal of a prescribed procedure of peaceful settlement. There seems to me to be a very serious danger in leaving the matter wholly to the determination of the Security Council, as the Charter does, with nothing to ensure that the determination will be just except its general obligation to act in accordance with the Purposes and Principles of the United Nations. For it has been quite justly pointed out that there is nothing in the Charter to preclude the Security Council from deciding that a threat to the peace would most conveniently be met by another Hoare-Laval or Munich solution at the expense of a weak Power.

A necessary corollary of the co-operative principle on which the Covenant was founded was the so-called 'rule of unanimity', and many not always well informed critics have seized on this as a capital instance of a weakness in the Covenant which it was essential to remove. Generally the argument has proceeded on *a priori* lines. Since Article V had declared that 'except where otherwise provided...decisions at any meeting of the Assembly or of the Council shall require the agreement of all the members of the League represented at the meeting', this *must* have paralysed the League; therefore it did paralyse it. At San Francisco the Great Powers in a formal declaration even went so far as to claim that in this matter the Covenant was more stringent than the Charter, inasmuch as the Security Council, which was to be subject to the veto of only the Great Powers, would be less subject to obstruction than the League Council was with its requirement of complete unanimity. This was an astonishing statement, for the comparison was wholly fallacious, and I think it may help to an understanding of the real nature of the League and of the difference between the principles on which it and the United Nations are based, if we ask why it was that the rule of unanimity did not in fact paralyse the League.

There was more than one reason. In the first place there were important exceptions to its operation, especially the provision in Article XV that the votes of the parties were not to be counted for the purpose of unanimity when the Council made its report and recommendations on a dispute. Secondly, the practice of the League developed certain conventions which mitigated the operation of the rule in important respects. But the really fundamental reason was that the effectiveness of the League as a going concern did not depend upon its organs being able to reach decisions, but on the observance by the individual members of their obligations under the Covenant. It is true that decisions of the Assembly or the Council did often lead to the members taking joint action of various kinds, but no decision could alter or add to the obligations of a member against that member's will. The real effect of the rule was to prevent a member being forced to accept some addition to the obligations by which it was already bound under the Covenant. There were very few cases in which it was used as a veto to hold up action. I think the only one of serious consequence was when Japan used the rule to block a resolution on her own conduct in Manchuria in 1931, and this was only possible because of an unexpected and doubtfully correct ruling by the lawyers that under Article XI there was nothing to exclude the vote of an interested party. If the ruling was correct, it was almost certainly due to an error of drafting, and it would not have been acquiesced in if the Council had not been glad to be thus provided with an excuse for inaction.

But decisions under the Charter have a wholly different function from decisions under the Covenant; they are necessary in order to make the Security Council work at all. Hence it was absolutely necessary to provide against the possibility of deadlocks, and this could only be done by introducing some form of majority voting. That had become inevitable once it had been decided to abandon, as a weakening factor, the Covenant system of States binding themselves individually to act in certain specified ways and instead to confer a power of directing how they should act upon an organ of the collective body. Thus the crucial Article is Article XXIV: 'In order to ensure prompt and effective action by the United Nations, its members confer on the Security Council primary responsibility for the maintenance of international peace and security, and agree that in carrying out its duties under this responsibility the Security Council acts on their behalf.'

Now undoubtedly, so long as we are considering principles of political organization in the abstract and not the context in which a particular political organization will have to work, this change is the first and necessary step towards the formation of what the American Constitution calls 'a more perfect union'. If, indeed, a corporate body is to act, it is the only way, as the Charter says, 'to ensure prompt and effective action'. But for this advance there has been a price to pay, and the question is whether it has not been too heavy. The price is the veto of the Permanent Members of the Security Council.

In speaking of the veto I shall not dwell on the uses to which it has been put in the short experience that we have of the working of the United Nations. Most of us, I suppose, would say that it has been gravely abused by the Soviet Government on numerous occasions, but that is a matter which is not relevant to my argument. If we have patience, we may eventually get an arrangement, such as that which Mr Bevin recently proposed without success, which will prevent its use in a manner which violates both the spirit and the letter of the declaration which the Great Powers, including Soviet Russia, made at San Francisco. But the important question seems to me to be whether, even assuming an arrangement to limit the use of the veto, in accordance with the San Francisco declaration, to decisions which 'may have major political consequences and require enforcement measures', we shall not, even so, find that the price has been too high, and that the union which the Charter has given us is in the result even less perfect than that which we had under the Covenant.

It is certain and, I think, it is now generally understood, that the veto has made it impossible that enforcement measures should ever be taken against a Great Power. That means that in 1935, if the Covenant had contained a similar provision, Italy could, and of course would, have vetoed the taking of sanctions against herself, and she would have been free, so far as the Covenant was concerned, to proceed undisturbed with her aggression against Ethiopia. But to-day the only event which can seriously endanger the peace of the world is the aggression of a Great Power, and a system which solemnly declares, as the Charter does, that its purpose is 'to take effective collective measures for the prevention and removal of threats to the peace and for the suppression of acts of aggression', and yet does not propose to deal with aggression by a Great Power, is, I venture to say, not a system of collective security at all. Of course it may be that no system can deal with that case, and this seems to be the view taken by the official British Commentary on the Charter. 'It is imperative', it says, 'that the consent of the Great Powers should be necessary to action in cases in which they are not a party, since they will have the main responsibility for action. It is also clear that no enforcement action by the Organization can be taken against a Great Power itself without a major war. If such a situation arises the United Nations will have failed in its purpose and all members will have to act as seems best in the circumstances.... The creation of the United Nations is designed to prevent such a situation from arising by free acceptance by the Great Powers of restraints upon themselves.' All that may be true. But if it is, it seems hardly fair that the Preamble of the Charter should declare that the peoples of the United Nations have 'determined to unite their strength to maintain international peace and security'. What they have done, according to the Commentary, is something quite different.

Perhaps after all, however, the explanation of the Commentary is an afterthought. For if there never was any idea that the procedure of the Charter might, if necessary, be used against a Great Power, why do we need all those elaborate provisions which are contained in Chapter VII on 'Action with respect to Threats to the Peace'? It really does not make sense to suppose that all the members are to make armed forces available to the Security Council on its call, that they are to hold air force contingents immediately available for combined international action, that a Military Staff Committee is to advise the Security Council on all questions relating to its military requirements, and so on, if the only purpose of all these carefully thought out preparations is to deal with a Small Power when it misbehaves. Small Power aggression has never been, and cannot be, a serious problem if the Great Powers are agreed among themselves, and if they are not, then this machinery cannot be used.

Much the most probable explanation of the impasse at which we have arrived seems to me to be historical. I suspect it has resulted from the mood which prevailed at the moment when the Charter was made. Both the Covenant and the Charter reflect conditions which were existing at the time of their drafting; it was inevitable that they should, but the authors of the Covenant, by concentrating on the bare essentials, and leaving ample room for the League to grow, made this limitation of their outlook a less serious handicap than it is in the Charter. Still the weak points in both become more intelligible when we remember the contemporary circumstances. The Covenant was made after the First World War had ended, but when its lessons, or what then seemed to be its lessons, were still vividly present to the minds of its authors. There was a case for thinking that in 1914 the world had stumbled into a war which no one had really desired or intended; most men everywhere were peacefully inclined, but there had been obstacles which had prevented their desires from finding expression, and if these could be removed, peace might be made secure. Hence there should be open diplomacy and publicity for the engagements to which statesmen committed their nations; provision for delaying the outbreak of a threatened war in the belief that war delayed would probably be war averted; reduction of armaments because sooner or later the piling up of armaments must lead to their being used; and if war should come in spite of all these precautions, then it would probably be enough to rely on the economic weapon, whose decisive effects the recent war seemed to have proved, and the use of military sanctions might be relegated to the hazy background.

The Charter on the other hand was shaped at Dumbarton Oaks in the autumn of 1944, when the issue of the Second World War was still uncertain, and to outward appearance at least Germany and Japan still seemed immensely strong. It sought to forge a weapon which could be used against just such a danger as then existed if history should ever repeat itself, a security system of irresistible power, and ready, as the Allies in 1939 had not been, for immediate action, and every other consideration was subordinated to this overriding purpose. No one believed that we had merely stumbled into the War of 1939; it had obviously been deliberately planned, and against a planned war the palliatives of the Covenant seemed a puny defence. Unfortunately, the weapon which was fashioned has turned out to be a highly specialized instrument, useful only against a particular danger for which we now no longer need it, and only on the assumption that the war-time unity of purpose among the Great Powers would be a permanent feature of their relations. In the circumstances then it seems a little odd that the one danger which the Charter system does seem well fitted to deal with, a revival of aggressive tendencies in Germany or Japan, should have been excluded from the sphere of the Security Council and left, by Article LIII, to be dealt with by regional arrangements. Thus the desire for a system of security ready always for immediate action, which was the leading motive behind the substitution of the Charter for the Covenant, has resulted in a system that can be jammed by the opposition of a single Great Power. Under the Covenant the League might be unable to act as a League, but at least the members of the League could act together if the occasion demanded joint action. The members of the United Nations cannot even do that; a Great Power can forbid it. The Covenant scheme had weaknesses, as I have already admitted, and perhaps it might not have worked even if it had been given a fair trial; if so no doubt it is better that we should know where we stand, as I think we do to-day. But we must realize that what we have done is to exchange a scheme which might or might not have worked for one which cannot work, and that instead of limiting the sovereignty of States we have actually extended the sovereignty of the Great Powers, the only States whose sovereignty is still a formidable reality in the modern world.

This is a depressing conclusion, and I do not want to end my comparison on a purely de-structive note. For I think there is a moral to be drawn. It is common ground, I think, among all of us who recognize the urgency of a better inter-national order that a condition of the stabilization of peace is some limitation of the sovereignty of States. We may not all use that phrase in quite the same sense, but at least there is a large measure of agreement about the ultimate aim. But there are differences amongst us as to methods, and I think the choice lies between the method of a frontal attack on sovereignty and what I may call the method of erosion. The Charter has tried to proceed by the former of these, and it has found the road barred. It insisted that to act effectively an international organization must have the power to make decisions, which means that a majority must be able to overrule a minority. But the Great Powers have refused to be outvoted. I know that the Charter has introduced majority voting into the General Assembly as well as into the Security Council, and that the Great Powers have not insisted on a veto over the decisions of the former. But this only reinforces the lesson which I think we have to learn. The General Assembly cannot act for all its members as the Security Council can, and this makes all the difference. Its decisions are not directions issued by the Organization to the member States to tell them what they are to do. Apart from its control of the Budget, all that the General Assembly can do is to discuss and recommend and initiate studies and consider reports from other bodies. In principle its functions are similar to those of the Assembly of the League; it must rely on co-operation among the members and not on power, for it has no powers. Hence the rule allowing it to take its decisions by majority voting was no very serious innovation in international organization. The case is entirely different when it has been decided that an international body shall exercise power, as the Security Council is to do. Then you are departing from the co-operative principle which has hitherto been the basis of international institutions; you are introducing a genuinely governmental element into them, converting the organization from a 'they' into an 'it'. To my mind the moral of the veto is that it teaches us that before international institutions can be raised from the co-operative to the organic type, which in itself is a desirable aim for which we have to work, we need a society far more closely integrated than the society of States is to-day; we need a society whose members have the same sort of confidence in one another's intentions and policies and the same absence of fundamental diversity of interests that the States of a federation must have if their union is to endure. I do not myself feel that in present world conditions the insistence of the Great Powers on their veto, however much we may deplore it, is altogether unreasonable, and I do not think that any system of weighted majority voting will induce them, or at any rate induce all of them, to change their attitude. I think we have been led into a cul-desac by the over-hasty pursuit of a perfectionist policy, and by a too shallow diagnosis of the causes of failure of the League. By insisting that only an institution which has power to decide can act effectively we have created one that can neither decide nor act.

What I have called the method of attacking sovereignty by erosion is less spectacular, but, I think, more likely to give results. It means doing everything we can to make it easy for States to work together and so gradually develop a sense of community which will make it psychologically more difficult to press the claims of sovereignty in ways that are anti-social. This was the method of the League, and for a time at least it did seem to be leading to results. The Charter has made it more difficult by making the sessions of the Security Council continuous and excluding all but questions of security from its sphere. Many of the causes of embitterment of recent months would never have been raised if the Security Council had not provided a too tempting sounding board for ideological invective; to raise them in diplomatic notes would not have been worth while. For our hopes for the United Nations we must look, I think, to the General Assembly, and more especially to the Economic and Social Council which in effect is one of its committees.

More obviously to-day, though not more certainly, than ever before, peace depends on the ability of the Great Powers to work together. In a sense I think we have returned, as I have seen it somewhere suggested, to the idea which underlay the Concert of Europe in the nineteenth century. We have failed to institutionalize the preservation of peace, and perhaps we have to recognize that that cannot be done. But it is something that we should face the future, as I think we now do, with a fairly general realization of where we stand. A generation ago the number of those who both believed that the League was tremendously important and also saw that the difficulties in its way were immensely formidable was not very large; too many of those who thought it important underrated the difficulties, and too many of those who saw the difficulties had no particular wish to see it make good. I think the present attitude of public opinion is more healthy. There is no disposition to look upon the United Nations as a beneficent power which will usher in the millennium without any effort on our part, and the pseudo-realism of those who thought that we had had to accept the League in order to humour President Wilson has also disappeared. It is true, as Lord Cecil has somewhere pointed out, that whereas the League was imposed on the governments from the outside, the United Nations is the work of the governments themselves. The only realist to-day is the man who knows that somehow we have got to use it to create a more civilized international order, and that probably we may not have very long in which to do it.